The Flower Girl

by
N. L. Sharp

illustrated by
Timothy James Hantula

Published by Prairieland Press
PO Box 2404
Fremont, NE 68026-2404
Printed in the U.S.A.

Original Book Design by Lynn Gibney

ISBN-10: 0-97598290-7
ISBN-13: 978-0-97598290-7

Prairieland Press™

For my sisters, Charliss and Corliss,
and all of our princesses.

—*N. L. Sharp*

Sophie *loved* flowers. She loved real flowers and fake flowers and flowers in fields. She loved pink flowers and purple flowers and yellow flowers. She even loved to eat flowers. Candy flowers and cookie flowers and cauliflowers. So she wasn't surprised when her mom said she was going to be the flower girl in her Uncle Dan's wedding.

"What does a flower girl do?" Sophie asked.

"You walk down the aisle, carrying a basket of rose petals," Mom said.

"What happens if I drop it?" Once, she was carrying a bowl of water for her cat, Max. It tipped, and water splashed all over the living room floor.

"Don't worry," Mom said. "You're supposed to drop the petals. That way, the bride will have a path to follow as she walks down the aisle."

"Do I have to wear a flower costume?" Sophie asked.

"No. You'll wear a dress," Mom said. "A sparkly white dress with lace and beads and flowers in your hair."

Sophie smiled. I'll look just like a princess, she thought. This was going to be fun!

Sophie wanted to be the best flower girl she could, so she practiced every day. She curtsied to her mom. She danced with her dad. And she marched around the garden with a bowl of cereal, sprinkling it on the grass so Max would have a path to follow.

Finally, there was only one day left before the wedding.

"Sophie, it's time to go to the church," Dad said.

"Why are we going there?" Sophie asked.

"We're going to practice our parts for the wedding, so tomorrow we'll know just what to do."

"I've been practicing," Sophie said. "Every day."

"Good," Dad said. "I'm proud of you. But tonight, Uncle Dan wants everyone to practice together."

Sophie looked at her clothes. "Where's my dress?" she asked.

"Here it is." Mom took a box out of the closet.

She helped Sophie slip the dress over her head.

Sophie stared at herself in the mirror. "Do I really get to wear this?" she asked.

"Yes," Mom said.

"Where's my crown?" Sophie asked.

"Here." Mom placed a wreath of flowers on her head.

Sophie twirled around in front of the mirror.

"Look at me," Sophie said. "I'm a princess. A beautiful, flower princess."

"Take it off," Mom said. "We don't want to get it dirty before tomorrow." She hung the dress back in the closet.

Soon it was time to go. Sophie was so excited, she could hardly sit still while they drove down the street. And when Dad stopped the car, Sophie couldn't believe her eyes. The church looked just like a castle!

There was a boy standing in front of the church. "This is Robert," Mom said. "You're going to walk down the aisle with him."

"Are you my prince?" Sophie asked.

"I'm no prince!" said Robert. "I'm the ring bear."

"A bear?" Sophie asked. "I have to walk down the aisle with a bear?"

"Yes," said Dad. "Didn't you know?"

"No!" said Sophie. "How can I be a princess if I'm walking with a bear?"

"You're not going to be a princess," Dad said. "You're going to be a flower girl."

Sophie shook her head. "*No!*" she said. "*I won't.* I want to be a princess. If I can't be a princess, I'm not going to be in the wedding!"

"You have to be in the wedding," Mom said. "Uncle Dan is counting on you."

"Someone else can drop the petals," Sophie said.

"I don't want someone else," Uncle Dan said. "I want you."

Sophie sat down on the curb. She thought about how much fun it had been practicing to be a princess. Then she thought about how sad Uncle Dan looked when she said she wasn't going to be in his wedding.

"Is it true you need someone to make a path for the bride to follow?" she asked.

"Yes, Sophie, it is," Uncle Dan said.

"And do you really want me to be the one to do it?"

"Yes," he said. "It wouldn't be the same without you."

Sophie curtsied. "All right," she said. "I'll do it."

The next day, Sophie wore her long white dress with a wreath of flowers in her hair.

She walked down the aisle dropping petals for the bride to follow. And everyone agreed, she was the ***best flower girl*** they had ever seen.

Later, at the reception, she curtsied to her mom.

She danced with her dad.

And she marched around the tables with a bowl of confetti, sprinkling it on the floor so that Robert, her ring bear prince, would have a path to follow.

And everyone agreed, she was the
best flower princess
they had ever seen, too.

Check out Robert's experience as the ring bearer in this wedding!

The Ring Bear

by
N. L. Sharp

illustrated by
Timothy James Hantula